*Coffee Time*

# An Artist's

# Pictorial Journey

'Petalaciously' yours in Paintings and Poems
by
Tina Bone

© Tina Bone August 2023

Coffee Time:

AN ARTIST'S PICTORIAL JOURNEY

*'Petalaciously' yours in Paintings and Poems*

by

Tina Bone

*Written, Edited and Illustrated by Tina Bone.*

Copyright © 2023:
Tina Bone UK (Tina's Fine Art UK)

All rights reserved. No part of this book may be reproduced, stored in a retrieval system, or transmitted in any form or by any means, electronic, electrostatic, magnetic tape, mechanical, photocopying, recording or otherwise, without permission in writing from the Author
(email: ourbooks@tinasfineart.uk).

PAPERBACK **118** pp.
ISBN No. 978-1-9168781-1-2
**58** Coloured Plates (129 illustrations in all)

Published by: Tina Bone UK
First published: **August 2023**

**https://tinasfineart.uk**
**Email: tina@tinasfineart.uk**

**Tina Bone**
**Wildlife & Botanical Illustrator**
**& Publisher**
**18 Harbour Avenue**
**Comberton**
**Cambridge CB23 7DD**

In memory of my wonderful mum—always remembered

## *Dedication*

To my loving husband, David, our three sons, Peter, Jason and Paul,
my two gorgeous sisters, Rosemary and Suzanna,
and my dear friend and co-author, Sylvia Haslam.

*Also, to all those wonderful people all over the world who have
purchased my paintings, prints, cards, calendars, diaries and jigsaw puzzles.
Since 2005 you have helped me to rekindle my passion for painting
and I am truly indebted to you all for loving my art and
contributing to my success in a second career.
Thank you so much.
TB*

FRONT COVER PICTURE:

'Pearly King and Queen' (Great Crested Grebes)

With swirling rhythm, flicking heads
They court and dance on bistort beds
As bubbles spray and sprinkle pearls
Golden neck plumes shine in whorls
Soon the babes on backs will ride
Stripey fluff-balls, sunnyside!

Artist Code: 1106. Completed July 2011. Original SOLD. Water colour on Aquarelle Arches 100% hot pressed cotton rag paper. Unframed size 12" x 16". Great Crested Grebes, *Podiceps cristatus*, amongst Amphibious bistort, *Polygonum amphibium*. This painting was selected for the National Exhibition of Wildlife Art (NEWA 2012). Sold at the Spring Exhibition, Natural World Art Group (NWAG), Banham Zoo, April 2013. Featured on the Publicity Poster for the Association of Animal Artists' Exhibition, at the Wildfowl and Wetlands Trust Martin Mere, Martin Mere Wetland Centre, Burscough, Lancashire L40 0TA, from 3 December 2013 to 23 February 2014.

# Acknowledgements

My heartfelt thanks to the wonderful people who have helped to make the painting of some of my pictures possible—too many to acknowledge singularly but every resource and permission is very much appreciated.

Many of my paintings have been produced using resources from my own stock of photographs and gifts of frozen specimens and road kills, and sketches from field trips. But, unfortunately, as I am not a 'globetrotter', exotic resources, and British animals and plants I have been unable to see, have had to come from other sources.

I am indebted and most grateful to those myriad individuals and institutions who have very kindly provided resources so that the pictures I have designed and painted are as true to the subject as possible. Without their consent to use photographs and specimens, many of my paintings would not have come to fruition.

Thank you everyone
TB

# Contents

Introduction .................................................................................................................. 1

'The Ladies are Listening' (Nightingales) ................................................................ 2

Gallic or French Rose ............................................................................................... 4

Evening primrose (Oenothera biennis) .................................................................... 6

'Tayabak' with Critters (Jade Vine) .......................................................................... 8

Flowering rush (*Butomus umbellatus*) ................................................................... 10

Pink Hollyhock (*Alcea rosea*) ................................................................................ 12

August Jay (*Garrulus glandarius*) .......................................................................... 14

Pink Pearls on a Velvet Cushion (*Rhododendron* 'Pink Pearl') ............................. 16

'Fruit of the gods': a theme in the various (Persimmon, Sharon fruit—*Diospyros kaki-Fuyu*) ...... 18

White Helleborines and Chiffchaffs (*Cephalanthera damasonium* and *Phylloscopus collybita*) ...... 20

*Beallara* Orchid Tahoma 'Glacier Green' (Hybrid Orchid) .................................... 22

Red Admirals and 'Woody' (Great Spotted Woodpecker) ...................................... 24

Birthwort (*Aristolochia gigantea*) .......................................................................... 26

Nature's Gems: May Kingfisher (*Alcedo atthis*) .................................................... 28

Passion Flower Bits (*Passiflora cerulia*) ................................................................ 30

Flag Iris and Friends (*Iris versicolor*) .................................................................... 32

Peaches and Blossom (var. unknown) .................................................................... 34

Hmm, nice trill! (Wrens in Foxgloves) ................................................................... 36

Garden of Lilies: Orange Lily (var. unknown) ....................................................... 38

Garden of Lilies: Milky Yellow Lily (var. unknown) ............................................. 40

Garden of Lilies: Alan's Red Lily (var. unknown) ................................................. 42

Winter Leaves at Wicken Fen (Long Eared Owl) .................................................. 44

Slipper Orchid II of V (*Paphiopedilum*) ................................................................ 46

Slipper Orchid V of V (*Paphiopedilum*) ................................................................ 48

The Sentinel Yearling (Young Roe Deer) .............................................................. 50

Marsh Marigold (*Caltha palustris*) ........................................................................ 52

Song Thrushes in Ivy .............................................................................................. 54

Brown Orchid: *Zygopetalum* .................................................................................. 56

Fritillaries and dew drops ....................................................................................... 58

Bird of Paradise (*Strelitzia*) .................................................................................... 60

Canoodling in the Loquats (Golden Orioles and Loquats) ..................................... 62

Roe Deer and Fawn at Fullers Mill ............................................................................................................64

Fullers Mill, West Stow, Suffolk. Iceni Botanical Artists Project to paint a year at Fullers Mill Garden......66–76

      Galanthus 'Queen Olga' (*Galanthus reginae-olgea*) ...............................................................66

      Galanthus 'Three Ships' (*Galanthus plicatus* subsp. *byzantinus*) ..........................................68

      Galanthus 'Richard Ayres' ......................................................................................................70

      *Galanthus 'gracilis'* ................................................................................................................72

      *Magnolia stellata* 2 (Star Magnolia).......................................................................................74

      *Clerodendrum trichotomum* 'Purple Blaze' (Harlequin Glory Bower) ....................................76

Little Explorers at the Mini Mart (Long tailed tits and Stinking Hellebore) ...............................................78

A House in Provençe .................................................................................................................................80

Three New Blades (Fieldfares and Redwing) ............................................................................................82

Dahlia: Bishop of Llandaff .........................................................................................................................84

Golden Pheasants and Bluebells ................................................................................................................86

*Iris bucharica* (Corn Leaf Iris) ..................................................................................................................88

Love at First Sight (Kingfishers, Reeds and Daisies) .................................................................................90

*Prunus* 'Mirabelle' (Yellow Plum) .............................................................................................................92

I Bow to my Queen (Turtle Doves) ............................................................................................................94

The Victorian Aviary Garden (2010 Chelsea Flower Show Garden).........................................................96

Flame Lily (*Gloriosa superba Rothschildiana*) ........................................................................................98

The Frank Taylor Memorial Peace Garden, Gardening World Cup 2010 ................................................100

'The Jay's Feather' (*Rhododendron ponticum*, white Japanese Anemones) ............................................102

Puffins and Thrift ('*Fratercula arctica* Antics') ......................................................................................104

The Mighty Reed with Fragility (Reedlings and Reeds) ..........................................................................106

Three Plucked Petals (Japanese Anemones, *Anemone hupehensis*).........................................................108

Torrid or Torrential—A brook in transit: the meandering Bourn (poem to be included in a book about Bourn Brook, Cambs, to be published under the "River Friend" series of Books by Tina Bone and Sylvia M. Haslam Website: https://riverfriend.tinasfineart.uk) ...........................................................................................110

# Introduction

*An Artist's Pictorial Journey*

*'Petalaciously' yours in Paintings and Poems*

*(An artist's artwork journey through
botanical, nature, and garden painting stories)*

Welcome dear Reader: this little book is intended as a 'light' read to lighten your mood and help you to enjoy some of the most wonderful plants, nature, and gardens, via my humble painting palette, in the comfort of your favourite armchair with a nice cup (or glass) of something. I do hope you enjoy the pictures as well as the [some] nonsense-poems and scripts. I just wish to share my paintings with others who may feel, by visual 'repast', a fraction of the great joy I experienced in producing them.

I have been painting professionally since March 2005, during which time I have enjoyed much success at local and national exhibitions, and with commissioned artwork. My paintings have sold worldwide.

Tina Bone<br>
September 2023

# The Ladies are Listening

At Paxton Pits, I guarantee
Live Nightingales, both she and he
The ladies timid in the bush
Dishevelled from migration's rush
Oh sing sweetly, nightingale sing
The ladies like your piccolo-ping
You've travelled far to sing your song
And hens have always tagged along
A little-brown-job with chestnut coat
Don't sing too loud; You'll get a sore throat!
(And other birds will start to gloat)
This singing star belts out his song
He'll win his girl before too long!

The design and execution of this natural history picture was one that required a lot of thought regarding the search for resource material and finding out about the bird and its habitat. But it has helped me to compose what I like to think is a natural scene, of which we are having a private view. The original was painted to provide a picture of Nightingales for The Friends of Paxton Pits Nature Reserve to produce greetings card which, together with some handcrafted coasters (see below right) were on sale in the Visitor Centre shop.

At a time around 2012 when internet pirates were being rather unscrupulous with copyright of artwork, I received a request for this painting to be used as a backdrop to a music festival in the US. I was rather afraid this was a scam, even though the person involved appeared to be a reputable musician. By the time I had made up my mind that it was not a scam she had found something else! What a missed opportunity—which still haunts me occasionally.

I eventually donated the painting to charity to raise funds for brain tumour research.

Artist Code 1015. (Later also called 'The Singing Nightingale'.) Water colour (12" × 16", completed March 2010). Nightingale—*Luscinia magarhynchos*, Ladybird—*Adalia bipunctata*, Hawthorn—*Crataegus laevigata*, Brimstone butterfly—*Gonepteryx rhamni*, Green hairstreak butterfly—*Callophrys rubi*, Bramble—*Rubus fruticosus*, Teasel—*Dipsacus fullonum*.

# Gallic or French Rose

Pink-on-pink is a 'girly' trend
For female garb is marked as 'friend'
As blooming roses, none compares
With nature's frills v. 'barby' wears
My description 'Petalacious'
Might be a bit fallacious
The gently moulded fronds of silk
With golden dustlets centre milk
For bees a buzzing scrambling round
Until sweet nectar can be found
As autumn sees the petals fall
A juicy rosehip forms the ball
As winter sets most plants to rest
Blood-red hips for fauna fest
Hanging on the branch with thorn
And winter hedges all adorn

This is one of four water colour artworks specially painted for the Society of Botanical Artists 'Arts Butanica' Exhibition at the Luton Hoo Walled Garden, which ran from 30th October to 6th November 2013.

The Exhibition was described as showing work by 22 of the UK's leading contemporary botanical artists. The exhibition and artworks were inspired by the records of the 3rd Earl of Bute, founder of the Luton Hoo Walled Garden. The History is that in 1785, John Stuart, 3rd Earl of Bute, a courtier, politician, patron of the arts and sciences, and enthusiastic botanist, decided to record his own botanical ideas. In the face of the new Linnean system of classification, Lord Bute published his 'Botanical Tables' in 12 sets of 9 volumes stating that the tables were 'composed solely for the amusement of the fair sex.'

*Many thanks to Cambridge University Botanic Gardens for providing the live plants for this particular project, and to Botanical Tutor, Petula Stone, for invaluable insights into the painting of this really bright pink flower which has a wonderful aroma.*

Artists Code 1307. *Rosa gallica*. Water colour painting on Aquarelle Arches 140lb 100% cotton rag paper size 12" × 16", completed October 2013.

# Evening Primrose

Evening Primrose has many a use
Its petals, not leaves, are very obtuse
The lemon yellow, simple blooms
Can swiftly ease some pains and glooms
Disease of heart, womb, stomach and breast
Its fragrant oil is much the best
It pales your troubles with just a few drops
In to your bath water with little plops
Then snuggle under suds galore
Your pains will ease, then you feel quite sure
That when the world is getting you down
A whiff of oil takes away that frown
A gentle plant with not much glamour
But a force for good in a gentle manner

Another of four water colour artworks specially painted for the Society of Botanical Artists 'Arts Butanica' Exhibition at the Luton Hoo Walled Garden, 2013.

Many thanks to my always-flower-supplier, my lovely neighbour Alan, for allowing me to pick his plant. An interesting exercise was that the plant came into flower too early for me to paint it, as I was still painting a flowering rush and a hollyhock, so I gave it a quick-freeze to see what would happen. The colours of the flowers and leaves remained perfect—but for about an hour only after they were removed from the freezer. This still gave me plenty of time to mix the right colour paint before the flowers and leaves turned a nasty black/brown colour! Incidentally, the brown fading on the lower leaves in the painting was natural decay and already happening when the plant was picked - it adds a nice piece of interest—as do the amiable water drops.

Artist Code 1306. *Oenothera biennis*. Water colour painting (12" × 16", completed October 2013).

# 'Tayabak' with Critters

Have you ever seen
such a lovely shade of green
A jade vine in all its glory
Flower bat in upper storey
Not from tropical forest, you'll pardon
But from Cambridge's Botanic Garden!
As Handsome Sunbirds spring and prance
Showing off their merry dance
Whilst butter-blue with emerald sheen
Amongst the blooms is hardly seen

'Tayabak' is the colloquial name for the beautiful Jade vine, which is now rare in the wild in its indigenous home in the Philippines. The plant grows beside streams in damp, tropical forests, or in ravines. But increasingly botanical institutions, which have discovered how to pollinate the flowers, have successfully grown this plant and it is now available for sale in garden centres. In the few places where the jade vine still grows in the wild, Philippine pygmy fruit bats fly amongst the 1m-long racemes, hanging upside down to suck the nectar from each flower and, as they do so, their heads touch the flower below and become coated with pollen. When they land on another bloom, the pollen on their heads falls onto a different flower and fertilization takes place. Handsome sunbirds and green barred swallowtail butterflies also live in or near the vine.

*My grateful thanks to Cambridge University Botanic Gardens for allowing me access to their beautiful flowering vine, which greatly helped in the design of this work. My grateful thanks also to my world-travelling friends for resource photographs of birds and butterflies. The background is by my own imagination.*

The painting was a finalist in The BBC Wildlife Artist of the Year (WAY) 2012 Award (Endangered Species category) and was also selected for the National Exhibition of Wildlife Art (NEWA) 2012, Catalogue Number 48.

(Similarly, a BBC WAY finalist in 2007, 'Jade Vine with Bat' (right) Artist Code 0701, completed in August 2006, was the original oil painting drawn on canvas life-size (12" x 48") in situ at the Cambridge Botanic Gardens. These field drawings were used again to help design and complete 'Tayabak' with Critters*.)

*Water colour (12" × 16", completed February 2012), Jade Vine—*Strongylodon macrobotrys*, Philippine pygmy fruit bat—*Haplonycteris fischeri*, Handsome sunbirds—*Aethopyga bella*, Green Barred Swallowtail Butterfly—*Papilio palinurus*. Artist Code 1201. Original sold at the Visual Arts Festival: Swaffham Rotary Art Exhibition, October 2014.

# Flowering Rush

There are many riparian pinky flowers
That can please an artist for many hours
When first I saw the Flowering Rush
I thought the flowers would easily crush
'Cause naughty me, with slight of hand
Absconded with it home to paint
Botanical study, very quaint
But wasted not the plant when done
As in my little pond, for fun,
I placed some seeds and a bit of root
And in the spring I saw a shoot
Although displaced, this dainty petal
Now lives in new tides in fine fettle

This is yet another of four water colour artworks specially painted for the Society of Botanical Artists 'Arts Butanica' Exhibition at the Luton Hoo Walled Garden, 2013.

*Butomus umbellatus* is a flowering plant loved by flies, hoverflies and butterflies in summer. It is a British native aquatic plant with long, triangular-shape leaves and pink flowers in umbels on tall stems. It grows to a height of between 60 and 90cm (24"–36"). The plant flowers June to July and grows from a rhizome (a clumpy-shape bulb with an irregular surface) in thick muddy substrate. Although this plant is called a Flowering 'Rush' it is not really of the rush family, but sits in its own botanical family called 'Butomaceae'.

Artist Code 1305. *Butomus umbellatus*. Water colour painting (12" × 16", completed October 2013).

# Pink Hollyhock

My usual source of specimens live
In Alan's garden boldly thrive
Of hollyhock there was no sign
I had to paint a study fine
So Alan looked both far and wide
And by the hedge the other side
Near privet bushes nicely growing
In Peter's garden in breezes blowing
This splendid Alcea so posey pink
Over driveway which made him think:
'Our artist friend can have all this —
By plants enraptured; she is in bliss'
So up it came with root and all
No longer was it growing tall
So Alan came back through the gap
Before the plant lost all its sap
And proudly brought it back to me
'There, paint this one', he said with glee

*(What fantastic neighbours!)*

This is the final painting of the four water colour artworks specially painted for the Society of Botanical Artists 'Arts Butanica' Exhibition at the Luton Hoo Walled Garden, 2013.

*My grateful thanks to Jenny and Peter for allowing Alan to pull up their lovely hollyhock so that I could draw and paint the whole plant, which incidentally did not sell at the SBA Exhibition. I next exhibited it at Swaffham Arts Festival in 2017 where it sold preview evening and I met the buyers who were over the moon with it and loved its intricacies.*

Artist Code 1304. *Alcea rosea*. Water colour painting (12" × 16", completed October 2013).

# August Jay

Oh Jay, Oh Jay, Oh Jay, Oh Jay!
I'm looking this—then that-a-way
Black elderberries, plump and juicy
Or crackling acorns, little beauties
Berries first because they're ready
Now don't be greedy, nice and steady!
Pink and white with buffy hue
And wings which flash with vivid blue
The startled jay's immediate flight
From danger is a wondrous sight
But when he sits amongst his food
That puts him in a braver mood!

A very rare visitor to my little wild garden, but spotted down the road a little way flitting between the small oak tree and elderberry and bramble hedge near a roadside ditch.

The Eurasian Jay (*Garrulus glandarius*) is part of the Crow family (Corvid), slightly leaner than the famed Jackdaw. As well as being very partial to elderberries, acorns and insects, it will also take what it can get, such as eggs and baby birds, bats and small rodents. During the day they are known to attack tawny owls which in turn predate on the Jay at night. Goshawks and Peregrine Falcons also like a bit of Jay. Its call is a rasping screech, but it is also a great imitator both of human-made sounds and other birds. Sometimes it is difficult to assess whether a Jay is making a noise unless you can see it because of all the imitation sounds it can make.

Whilst driving along Comberton Road, Hardwick (Cambs) in July 2014, suddenly a Jay flew across the road in front of me. I could not believe that it had a young blue tit in its beak—which was quite startling. So, even though they are beautiful birds to look at, they have a natural tendency to predate smaller bird species. And of course, that is just Nature, as that particular Jay probably had young to feed.

Water colour. Artist Code 0707. (12" × 16", completed September 2007). Jay—*Garrulus glandarius*, Acorns, Oak—*Quercus robur*, Elderberries—*Sambucus nigra*. Original sold at Marwell International Wildlife Art Society (MIWAS) 10th Annual Exhibition, August 2008.

# Pink Pearls on a Velvet Cushion

Outside the spring had long been coming  
Winter's cold refused to yield  
Then suddenly the bees were humming  
And bursting buds released their shield  
A pinky, pearly frilly swathe  
In late spring sunshine nicely bathed  
I sat it on a cushion fine  
And painted to my heart's design

By chance I saw an advertisement in *Artists & Illustrators Magazine* at the end of May 2013 regarding a call for entries for *The Sunday Times* Watercolour Competition 2013. It looked rather interesting so I thought I might make a submission. I popped outside to my little wild garden and noticed the beautiful pink rhododendron was just coming into flower. (This tree has been moved around in the garden so many times, and I cut it back harshly every year, it is a wonder it is still alive let alone flowering!). A title came into my head immediately: 'Pink Pearls on a Velvet Cushion' and I imagined a sprig of these lovely pink flowers sitting on a velvet cushion with a bit of gold braid. I spent the next ten days beavering away and managed to submit the painting online with a few hours to spare of the deadline - and this is the first time I have actually replicated on paper the picture that was in my head!

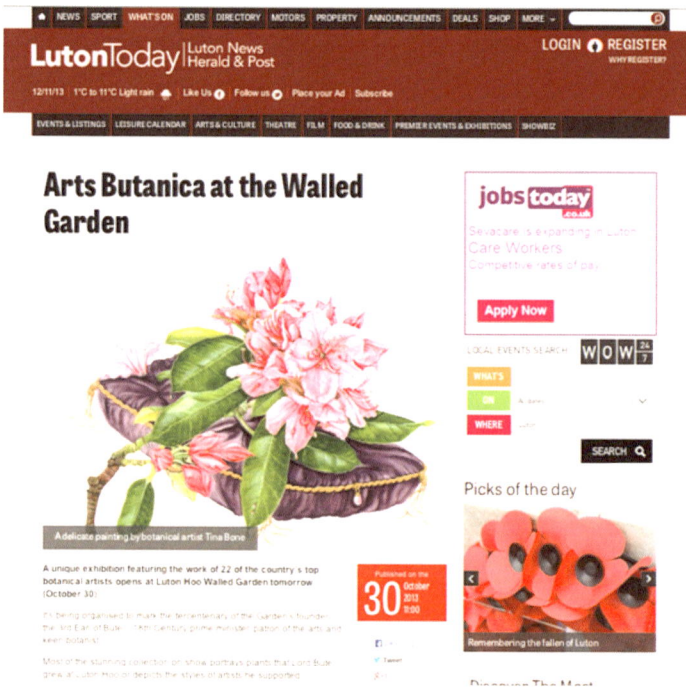

Unfortunately, the painting did not reach the contest finals—when I saw the accepted short list they were all very modern art—but I thoroughly enjoyed designing and painting it. After it failed to sell at several exhibitions, I donated it to a Charity Fund-raising day with all proceeds going to Milton Hospice for terminally ill children in Cambridge.

Artist Code: 1303. Water colour painting (9" × 12" completed August 2013). *Rhododendron* 'Pink Pearl'. This painting was selected by the Luton Hoo Walled Garden team to promote the SBA Arts Butanica Exhibition, October-November 2013. Featured on the LutonToday Website (*Luton News Herald & Post*) captioned: 'A delicate painting by botanical artist Tina Bone'.

# 'Fruit of the gods': a theme in the various

This golden orange globe of bliss  
Bathes the palate like a kiss  
No worldly noun its taste described  
Its fleshy juice and tales imbibed  
My lovely mum gave me this tree  
It nurtures her fond memory  

My mum gave me two Persimmon trees in the 1990s. I had 'tended' them by cutting them back fiercely each year to not upset my neighbour's garage foundations, and those of my own porch! In 2012 one of the trees flowered, and produced two fruits. The hard frosts of autumn meant that all the leaves and fruits were about to fall off the trees, so I just had to make a picture from the live specimens (having made a drawing of the flower earlier in the year, and now putting all the elements together).

In spring 2014 the same tree was absolutely covered in blossoms; but the second plant was yet to show any signs of flowering—it just produced wonderfully large leaves.

On 18 September 2013 I received a lovely email: 'Dear Tina, Would you mind if we use your lovely Persimmon on our latest promotional material? All the best, The Arts Team, Luton Hoo Walled Garden.'

This painting was also published on the front cover of the Arts Butanica Catalogue, in the advertisement for the exhibition on the bGallery Website, as well as featured on the HVA (Herts Visual Arts) Website.

Sadly, in 2021 both trees had to be removed because they were causing damage. But I still have the wonderful memories associated with them.

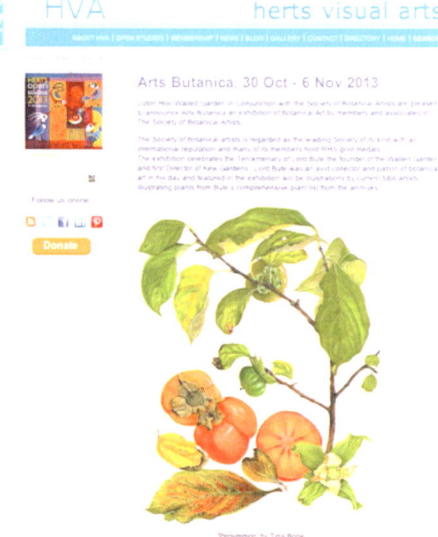
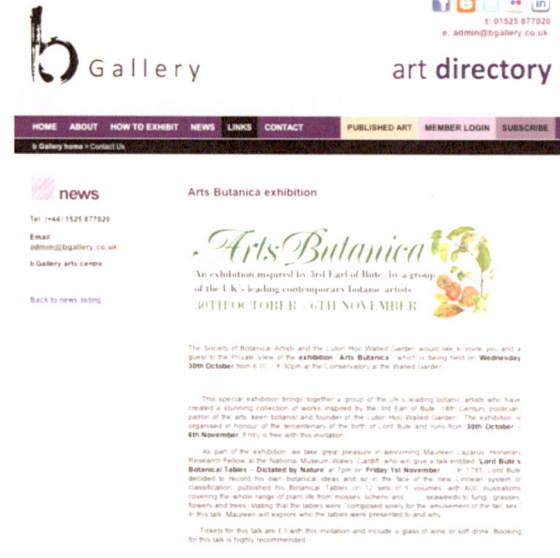

Water colour. Artist Code: 1212. (12" × 16", completed November 2012). Persimmon, Sharon fruit—*Diospyros kaki-Fuyu*.

# White Helleborines and Chiffchaffs

A friend did 'phone: 'Exciting news—
White helleborines in garden views'
I rushed to draw all *en plein air*
Was heartened by the beauty there
And all around with 'chiff-chaff' cries
The Chiffchaffs flit before my eyes!
Shy, aloof the Chiffchaff still—
Is not a bird of run-of-mill
You might espie at top of tree
Singing brightly for all to see
But calmness comes, her presence felt
His lot is cast, his hand is dealt

It just so happened that I had an evening tennis match at Great Shelford (Cambs) which dovetailed nicely with an invitation to visit a friend's wild garden near the Gog Magog Hills to draw White Helleborines *en plein air* which could not be refused. I packed up drawing materials in May 2010 and sat amongst these beautiful flowers in the afternoon sun, with chiffchaffs flitting about amongst the undergrowth, and trilling their unmistakable 'Chiff-Chaff, Chiff-Chaff' all around me. It was such an enchanting scene that, along with discarded pots tangled in the undergrowth, a composition was born (I am yet to paint a botanical illustration of the White helleborines!). I was allowed to pick a couple of stems, to help me with the fine art drawing. I also wished to portray the very-hard-to-see chiffchaffs in a natural environment. Although it looks as though the bottom bird is being encouraged to make a nest in the pot, this probably would not happen, as Chiffchaffs usually nest on the ground, making a sturdy ball nest of grasses and mosses. They are reasonably safe from predators because they are very shy, unobtrusive little birds (when they are not high up in the trees singing that is!). Many thanks to Valerie and John for the live plant material and for the use of their beautiful garden for inspiration.

Painters Online favourite image: 'I am writing to let you know that one of your paintings from the gallery at painters-online.co.uk has been chosen by the team as one of their favourite images added during July. As such the image will appear in a special panel on the home page of the site for the whole of August, and also on the page Gallery Images 2011. Congratulations on having your work chosen.'

Artist Code 1103. Water colour with gum arabic (12" × 16", completed March 2011). White helleborines—*Cephalanthera damasonium* (previously *Cephalanthera latifolia*), and Chiffchaffs—*Phylloscopus collybita*. Original sold at the National Exhibition of Wildlife Art (NEWA) 2011 exhibition. Wentworth Whimsy Jigsaw Puzzle from 2011 to 2014: www.jigsaws.co.uk, Catalogue no. 602506.

# Beallara Orchid Tahoma 'Glacier Green'

*'Luxury, Style and Elegance'*

Greek olden times were promiscuous
An orchid given was perspicuous
Victorians honed its beauty bare
Compared with delicate lady fair
An orchid given showed love, respect
A lasting bond to this effect

This painting was selected for the 2013 Society of Botanical Artists Exhibition, 'The Language of Flowers' and featured in the Exhibition Catalogue, Number 69. It was also featured on the SBA Website Gallery. The Victorians, in 'The Language of Flowers', used Orchids to symbolize a respectful love for a delicate lady.

My wonderful neighbour (who grows orchids and other exotic plants) came round on 28 July 2012 during my Cambridge Open Studios weekend bearing this beautiful orchid, and it took me two months to complete the portrayal. A Fifteen-hour, non-stop stint of drawing and composition produced a preliminary sketch. And 100 or so hours later the picture was completed. Usually the orchids are in a sorry state when I return them to my neighbour, but I am pleased to say that this one had actually grown a new shoot by the time it was returned to its cosy hot-house spot next door.

Artist Code 1208. Water colour (22" × 30", completed September 2012). Hybrid Orchid. The original of this large (life-size) painting was sold to an overseas buyer (Florida, USA).

# Red Admirals and 'Woody'

Even though his coat is bright
'Woody peck' can cause a fright
When startled by your passing by
He cackles as he starts to fly
He plugs his claws into his food
A comic, and a real cool dude!

I have many logs and branches in my little 20ft × 20ft wild garden and 'Woody' has taken to drumming away on some rotting beech logs where he grabs a grub and flits away. He is also partial to a few peanuts and other seeds from the bird feeders in the garden. There is an electricity pole, which looks like the old fashioned wooden telegraph poles, at the bottom of the garden and the bird sometimes scoots up and down it, also hunting for food in the nooks and crannies of the old wood.

Great Spotted Woodpeckers are slightly larger than a blackbird with striking black-and-white plumage, a buffy-red breast and bright scarlet patch below the breast underparts. It has a 'bouncing' flight but spends a lot of time clinging to tree trunks and branches, flitting from one side to the other to prevent a birder's good observation. Its loud, cackling call and spring 'drumming' display make this one of the loudest birds in the woods. The male has a red patch on the back of his head, whereas the female does not, and juveniles have a red crown, which eventually turns black as they mature.

The woodpecker's favoured habitat is deciduous woodland, especially where there are mature broad-leaved trees, but they also tolerate conditions in conifer forests. This bird loves to visit your peanut feeders and bird tables. It is quite common in England and Wales. They mostly eat insects, seeds and nuts, but are partial, as this picture shows, to the odd piece of crab apple and perhaps the red admirals gorging on the spiked, rotting crab apple in the picture might be at risk…?

Artist Code 0710. Water colour (12" × 16", completed October 2007). Original sold at National Exhibition of Wildlife Art (NEWA) 2008. Great Spotted Woodpecker—*Dendrocopus major*, Red admiral butterfly—*Vanessa Atalanta*, Crab apple—*Malus sylvestris*.

# Birthwort

The strange maroon flowers of this tropical climber attract insects into the entrance to the pouch behind the petal, where they are temporarily trapped to ensure they are covered in pollen before escaping to enter and fertilize another flower.

It is called 'birthwort' because of its historical medicinal use in childbirth. This family of plants contains aristolochic acid which has been shown to cause complete kidney failure. In 2001, the FDA (Food and Drug Administration, USA) issued a warning to consumers to immediately stop taking herbal medicines containing aristolochic acid.

I received a commission to paint five plants to feature in new ID signs at Marwell Wildlife's Tropical World in November 2009. I visited the zoo to meet the commissioners and to view the plants *in situ*. I took resource photographs and received live material of the plants. I had to submit preliminary drawings for approval and all were accepted with only one minor alteration.

'Marwell Wildlife seeks to address causes of extinction such as habitat loss and the over-exploitation of biological resources and to manage vulnerable populations of threatened species to ensure their survival. This is achieved through a range of species and habitat conservation programmes locally through Marwell's base in southern England and internationally, with a particular focus in Africa.'

[Commissioned Plants, below from Left to right:
ROSY PERIWINKLE *(Catharanthus roseus)*; FRINGED HIBISCUS *(Hibiscus schizopetalus)*; PASSION FLOWER *(Passiflora trifasciata)*; VANILLA ORCHID *(Vanilla planifolia variegata)*.

Artist Code 1012. Water colour (12" × 16", completed February 2010). *Aristolochia gigantea*. Genera: Aristolochiaceae. Origin: Brazil. One of five paintings commissioned by Marwell Wildlife, Colden Common, Winchester, Hants SO21 1JH (https://www.marwell.org.uk/). The 'Marwell Collection' was painted between January and March 2010.

# Nature's Gems: May Kingfisher

A fleeting rest, kingfisher blue
Amongst the brambles, out of view
Yellow flags rise tall and bright
As dazzling damselfly so light
Flits amongst the leaves of sedge
And other plants by water's edge
With tinselled spots upon his crown
And iridescent feathered down
This splendid bird with beak of might
Sits on his perch with eagle's sight
He plunges suddenly with speed
And catches fish amongst the reed

The kingfisher dashed passed whilst I was enjoying the sun in my little wild garden, he rested fleetingly on a bramble near my tiny wild pond (no fish), then whirled away out of sight. I sat wondering whether I had really just seen that! It has been back several times, but usually to my neighbour's (much bigger and huge) pond with fish, but still flies occasionally through my garden, and probably has a fleeting rest when I am not looking. What a beautiful bird.

Apparently the iridescent blue colour of the feathers of kingfishers is caused by light refracting against the actual brown-grey colouration of its feathers. As the light shines on the feathers, it 'bounces around' causing the iridescent plume. This is why, in both paintings and photographs, you can see such a variety of blue or green tints in the birds plumage.

Artist Code: NS05. Water colour (12" × 9", completed May 2004) Kingfisher—*Alcedo atthis*, Yellow Flag Iris—*Iris pseudacorus*, Blue Damselfly—*Libellula*, Lesser Pond Sedge—*Carex acutiformis*. Original sold at National Exhibition of Wildlife Art (NEWA) August 2008. Painted over a light yellow background wash.

# Passion Flower Bits

Passion Flower Bits, Planted near our boundary fence
Migrated to a neighbour's, whence, It promptly left
our fencing bare, We could only stand and share
It's beauty with our neighbour's gaze—
Foundations for our friendship lays.
I painted fruit and buds galore
I thought perhaps there should be more
But Judge in Show at SBA
Said it's lovely in this way
She gave the piece a seal of merit
Botanical Certificate I did inherit

This is one of five paintings exhibited at the Society of Botanical Artists 25th Anniversary Exhibition, Great Westminster Hall, London, April 2010, where it won a Certificate of Botanical Merit (CBM). It also featured in the printed March 2010 issue of *Artists & Illustrators Magazine* as image of the month in the Portfolio section.

The reasoning behind the name of this painting, which took two years to complete, is twofold: it is composed of bits of the plant and they come at different times of the year; and my original resource plant was dug up by the owner and thrown away by the next year, so I had to find another of the same species to complete it! Fortunately, one that had been sown in our garden many years ago which we thought had gone, actually sprung up in our neighbour's garden and grew through our bordering fence. I think you will agree, all parts of this propulsive climber have their own special beauty. There are many varieties of this plant, and I think this one is the most common in British gardens.

Artist Code 1003. Water colour (12" × 16", completed December 2009), Passion Flower, *Passiflora cerulia*. The original of this painting was sold to a private collector.

# Flag Iris and Friends

This life-size canvas, done with oils  
Points up Mother Nature's foils  
As hedgehog gollops slimy snails  
And worms in beak show some entrails  
With pleas for meals by mother's love  
The anxious fledgling looks above  

These beautiful flags used to grow under my other neighbour's hedge (not Alan!) and every year provided a wonderful splash of colour in the spring. Both our gardens shared the hedgehog. Robins nested in their territories nearby, and the fledglings hid and melded into all sorts of places—including the bulbous rhizomes protruding from the earth at the base of the plants (which need to be bleached by the sun in order to encourage flowering). Snails also lived amongst the protruding tubers which interlaced on the ground. Whilst I was sketching this picture I noticed a fledgling robin amongst the roots and its parent robin hopping about with little worms in its beak, so they both just had to be included in the final painting design.

This painting was sold before it was completed. I was using the painting to demonstrate how I paint in oils for visitors to my Open Studio in July 2010. A family came in with the intention of commissioning me to paint a portrait of the children. But the whole family liked the sketch and preliminary painting so much that they returned in October to purchase the completed artwork.

Sadly we do not get hedgehogs here anymore (2023); but the robins are still around and nest near by which is a consolation. We mostly have doves and pigeons in the garden now with the occasional blackbird and smaller goldfinches and tits.

Artist Code 1001. Lifesize oil painting on stretched canvas (36" × 28", completed September 2009). Flag Iris—*Iris versicolor*; Robin—*Erithacus rubecula*; Garden Snails—*Helix sp.*; Hedgehog—*Erinaceus europaeus*.

# Peaches and Blossom, var. unknown

A traditional Botanical Illustration  
The commissioner was in admiration  
A beautiful fruit with leaves and flowers  
To finish this painting took umpteen hours  
Dewdrops nestled on crinkled leaf  
And stone removed from fleshy sheath  
Pink blossom glows in sweet abundance  
By precious bees to fruits transcendence  
Then swelling by the autumn rain  
The hairy fruit its girth is gained  
And then we pluck it from the tree  
Are glad to eat it for our tea!

The live foliage and fruit for this commission were kindly provided by a near-neighbour, and I used an old resource photograph I had already to help with the blossom depiction as blossoms that year were long gone at the time I was asked to do the painting.

The commissioner was very happy with the painting which was commissioned as a birthday present for a very dear friend in China, so I had to look up the background regarding Chinese history and the peach and discovered that it was to indicate (and wish) longevity upon a particular person, and that all components, i.e. leaves, flowers, fruits etc., should be in odd numbers rather than even, and that the blossoms should show buds as well as fully-out blossoms to indicate nature's growing cycle. A truly wonderful painting experience.

Artist Code 1407. This wonderful commission was completed on 4th October 2014. Unframed size 12" x 16" Aquarelle Arches 100% cotton rag. The commission brief was to produce a very accurate botanical illustration of a peach, including ripe fruit, branch, blossoms and cross section.

# "Hmm, nice trill!"

At Incleboro' Fields one day  
The loudest shrill came into play  
With tail erect and beak astride  
He sat on foxglove with great pride  
She watched from down below in shade  
And hoped his song would never fade  

Whilst taking a short break in my caravan at Incleboro Fields Caravan Club Site, West Runton, Norfolk in May 2010, I decided to go for a quiet walk through the site, taking my camera with me. As I walked I could hear a loud piercing shrill and crept towards the sound. A bulbous little wren was singing his heart out, perched on top of a foxglove! I noticed the sunlight beaming across the scene, the white whispy clouds against a dark blue-mauve sky, and immediately wanted to paint a picture! However, in the few seconds it took me to put the camera to my eye, the wren saw me and flitted away out of sight.

Nevertheless, I snapped the foxglove and surrounding vegetation and remembered that I had a similar shot of a wren amongst my myriad photographs, and also found another couple of wren photographs, both being of the incumbent wren which lived at the time in my little wild garden. My grateful thanks to my neighbour, Alan, for allowing me to pick and use his foxgloves as live plant material.

This little painting has been very popular as a traditional jigsaw puzzle. I also designed my own puzzles: 'Diwejisaws', which are A4 size magnetic puzzles. I cut each piece by hand so they are all different, but all diamond shape pieces rather than the usual traditional shape.

*This is what the puzzle looks like before I cut it all up by hand along each line, both ways. The puzzles are sold with a magnetic base on which the puzzle is put together. Nimble fingers are required as the pieces are slid into place rather than clipped into place which gets some getting used to. The first time I made one (as a trial), it had larger pieces and I took it down to Marwell Zoo with me when I exhibited there as a member of the Marwell International Wildlife Art Society. I had a stand during the exhibition and had this puzzle on display to see what folk would make of it. Imagine my surprise (and complete delight) when an eight-year old girl saw it and started putting it together. Her mother was enthralled that her daughter was engrossed in the task. However, after about fifteen minutes the mother wished to move on—of course the girl did not. The mother asked if she could leave her daughter doing the puzzle and go off to see the rest of the exhibition. I was quite happy to 'babysit'. I am pleased to say that she completed the puzzle in just under an hour, by which time mother had returned. I gave the girl a greetings card of the wrens to remember her visit by. So the decision was made to make more...!*

Artist Code: 1108. Water colour (12" × 9", completed June 2011). Wrens—*Troglodytes troglodytes*, Foxgloves—*Digitalis*. Sold to private buyer and shipped to Singapore March 2016.

# *Garden of Lilies: Orange Lily*

Bright Orange lilies in summer garden
No beauty help from Elizabeth Arden!
Nature's mischievous colour balance
Dark brown tips versus apricot valence
With shining leaves that whorl around
The spotted stem as it dives to ground

This is the first of five paintings submitted to the Society of Botanical Artists in the second year of application to gain Membership. (The criteria was five paintings accepted for the annual open exhibition, two years' running, i.e. 10 out of 10 submitted paintings accepted over two successive years. The first set of five submitted paintings—orchids—is shown later in this book.) (I only managed 'Associate' membership as my work was not considered good enough. However, I was extremely pleased to receive a 'Certificate of Botanical Merit' in 2010 for my 'Passion Flower Bits' painting, already shown in this book!)

All five lilies were picked from my neighbour Alan's lovely garden, and the pictures were composed to show the character of each plant and to demonstrate the wonderfully different colours and textures of their flowers and leaves.

I ceased membership of the SBA in 2012 after my work increasingly was not selected for the exhibition and it was rather expensive to go down to Westminster Hall, London and back twice with artwork, especially when it was rejected. Since 2008, the criteria for becoming a member of the Society of Botanical Artists have changed—although the standard of work has continued to improve year-on-year.

Artist Code 0809. Water colour (9" × 12", completed July 2008). Orange Lily, var. unknown.

# Garden of Lilies: Milky Yellow Lily

Milky yellow, floral suede
No sheen upon the petals made
A bright red tip to stigma bold
And stamens green and subtle gold
With little spots towards the core
And bulging greeny buds galore
The whorling leaves of satin sheen
Hiding flower head once been
The dewdrops add a pretty sight
Lily fair for our delight

Number four in the series of five lilies, submitted to the Society of Botanical Artists to gain membership.

And my grateful thanks once again to Alan, my neighbour, for supplying the live specimens.

*Lily number 2 of 5*
*Yellow Lily*

*Lily number 3 of 5*
*Mauve Lily*

Artist Code 0812. Garden of Lilies: Milky Yellow Lily. Water colour (12" × 9", completed February 2009). Milky yellow Lily, var. unknown.

# Garden of Lilies: Alan's Red Lily (var. unknown)

Velvet silk with line indent
Spotted stalk just slightly bent
Green buds at the top in line
Disperse below to orange fine
Then blood-red blooms with stigma gleams
Surrounded by the stamen beams
And onwards down as leaves are whorled
Down to earth the plant unfurled

This lily had the good fortune to be chosen as one of the 16 designs to be produced by Ling Design on behalf of the Society of Botanical Artists range of greetings cards for three years from April 2011 to April 2014. Email from the SBA, received early December 2010: 'Congratulations your red lily has been selected as part of the SBA range.' (Ling Design—Publishers of Greetings Cards and Stationery. Contract for cards was for 3 years from April 2011, cards and notelets were available via Moonpig.com, Ling Design (wholesale) and at the Society of Botanical Artists Annual Exhibitions 2011 to 2014).

This painting is number five of five in a series.

And again my grateful thanks to Alan, my neighbour for supplying live specimens—I titled this particular painting in his honour!

Artist Code 0813. Water colour (9" × 12", completed August 2008). Red Lily, var. unknown.

# Winter Leaves at Wicken Fen

A long eared owl was spotted there
Amongst the willows, alders bare
As ancient windmill pump is still
The sunset-gold your heart does fill
As darkness falls the owl awakes
Silent loom, then prey it takes

The idea for this picture came to mind when I attended a caravan rally at Strumpshaw Steam Museum, Old Hall, Strumpshaw, Norwich NR13 4HR [www.strumpshawsteammuseum.co.uk] in May 2009. Hubby spent the days looking at steam engines and bygones, and I lost myself in the RSPB Strumpshaw Fen Nature Reserve. I saw the rippling trails of otters in the water, as they swam just below the surface scanning the waters for their next meal. As I walked back to base I noticed the leaf silhouettes against the lowering sun, and the black, shaded branches. Some leaves had holes and nibbled edges and they looked very wintry, even though it was late spring.

My grateful thanks to Howard Cooper, Communications Officer at Wicken Fen Nature Reserve who confirmed that a long eared owl had been spotted in the nature reserve at about the time I was designing this picture in my head, and he invited me to visit the reserve for further inspiration. Although the long eared owl was nowhere in sight, the combination of Strumpshaw silhouettes and the old wind pump at Wicken Fen amongst the reeded fenland landscape enlightened my mind. I used the old post and twigs from a photograph I had taken whilst at Wicken Fen to place my owl in the preliminary drawing of this composition. I did not refer to any of the photographs I had taken when painting it, so the landscape is entirely from my accumulated memories.

Many thanks to Paul Mason for lending me his taxidermed 'Owly', without which I would never have learned that the owl's facial feathers look like wire, his bib is like the soft down pulled from the belly of a mother rabbit when making her nest, and the wing and lower body feathers are so light and delicate, they are like a seed head of a dandelion telling the time—a symbol of possibility, hope, and dreams; and those eyes....

This picture was 'Image of the Month' for June 2011 at www.birdingart.com.

Artist Code 1105. Water colour painting (12" × 16", completed May 2011). Long Eared Owl—*Asio otus*, previously *Strix otus*. Original sold to private collector November 2015.

# Slipper Orchid 2 of 5

*Paphiopedilums*, number two of a set
I had to paint when first we met
Like leopard's skin—can't change its spots
It wasn't easy to paint these dots!
Thin lines and veins of different hue
Make up the whole and splendid view

This painting is number two in a series of five slipper orchids, painted for the Society of Botanical Artists Annual Exhibition in order to gain membership. This was the first set of five paintings submitted over two years. (The second set of five paintings submitted—Lilies—is listed earlier in this book.)

Preparation of the cotton rag paper on to which these five pictures were painted included applying several layers of light grey water colour wash, over which the drawing and painting was done, so that the delicate whites in the flowers, normally left as white paper, could be vividly represented.

A special set of A2 prints (4 × original size) of this painting were supplied to Project Art Ltd (Interior Designers, London, 'sourcing and supplying art for public and commercial space, exclusively with interior designers and architects'), who were very pleased with their prints produced in my studio, saying, 'Enclosed is a photo of your wonderful prints in their frames for our project…and we think they look really lovely…. they'll be hung in a palace in Saudi.' The painting was featured on their website on the Prints Gallery page.

Live material supplied, as usual, by my neighbour, Alan—as well as his well-stocked outside garden, he has a greenhouse and hot-house where he grows lots of lovely orchids.

Artist Code 0803. Water colour (12" × 9", completed November 2007). Slipper Orchid, var. unknown, *Paphiopedilum*. The original painting was selected for and sold at the 2008 Society of Botanical Artists' Exhibition, Westminster Hall, London.

# Slipper Orchid 5 of 5

*Paphiopedilums*, the last of five
I had to paint each plant alive
With frantic brush strokes—busy me
The deadline loomed, no time for tea!
Give thanks for five orchids fine
To share with all over given time

Number five of five slipper orchids, painted in 2008 to gain membership of the Society of Botanical Artists.

This painting was purchased later in the year in July at my Cambridge Open Studio event by a lovely young couple who were on honeymoon—the bride buying it with wedding-present money gifted to her. I was most humbled that a bride chose one of my paintings to grace her new London home.

Live material was, again, borrowed from Alan next door! I was so lucky that he had several beautiful orchids all flowering at once.

A special set of A2 prints of this painting was also commissioned by Project Art Ltd, for a 'Palace in Saudi'—thumbnail above.

*1 of 5 Artist Code 0802*     *4 of 5 Artist Code 0805*     *3 of 5 Artist Code 0804*

Artist Code 0805. Water colour (12" × 9", completed January 2008), Slipper Orchid, var. unknown, *Paphiopedilum*. The original painting was selected for the 2008 Society of Botanical Artists' Exhibition, Westminster Hall, London.

# The Sentinel Yearling

In fields of early August Mist  
Young Roe deer stands alert and tall  
With eyes that beam, so nothing's missed  
He watches, pertly, over all  
There's goldfinch, teasel, bindweed, sloe  
Scabious, hawthorn, with 'deer' little Roe!

The sketch right was produced in water-based oil colour on canvas whilst I was demonstrating my painting techniques in the Art Market Marquee at Marwell International Wildlife Art Society 2011 Exhibition (in conjunction with the BBC Wildlife Artist of the Year). The painted sketch was done *in situ* at the Exhibition, using natural plant material picked (with Landowners' permission) from the hedgerows in Hampshire, and the scene itself is a depiction of the wildlife (flora and fauna) seen whilst there. I spent so much time talking to people that I only managed to outline the sketch and paint a bit of background sky during the exhibition. It took almost a year after that to complete it—due to so many other commitments.

Artist Code 1207. Oil on stretched Canvas (18"× 24", completed June 2012). Roe Deer—*Capreolus capreolus*, Goldfinch—*Carduelis carduelis*, Hawthorn—*Crataegus monogyna*, Teasel—*Dipsacus fullonum*, Field Scabious—*Knautia arvensis*, Field bindweed—*Convolvulus arvensis*, Blackthorn (sloe)—*Prunus spinosa*. Original Sold at Hinchingbrooke Country Park Christmas Fayre November 2015.

# Marsh Marigold (Caltha palustris)

*Caltha palustris*, the Latin name
Bright yellow flowers of 'Kingcup' fame
Also is known as Marsh Marigold
Bright green leaves and buds behold
In marshy wetlands elegant flowers
On rivers edge 'neath willow cowers
In springtime swathes of beauty holds
As early sun makes buds unfold

This plant was used in church festivals in the Middle Ages, and on May Day festivals it was strewn at cottage doors and also made into garlands. Marsh Marigold, although a strong irritant, has many medicinal uses, including curing warts, preventing various kinds of fits, both in children and adults, and may be beneficial in cases of anaemia. The leaves can be cooked and eaten like spinach.

This is the first of several botanical plates for a book about rivers and river plants that I am co-authoring with Dr S M Haslam (Cambridge University). I messed up my first attempt at this painting and had to start again. It took 3 hours to re-trace the drawing onto good paper! I used a water colour pencil (different colours for different elements) on the back of the tracing so that the tracing would be very feint. However, upon pressing this onto the good paper I discovered the colour I had used for the stalks did not come out! So I drew these in by hand with a paintbrush—my favourite way to draw. It looked a bit messy, but was easily covered during painting. I added a seed head (not in the original sketch) because I took so long to paint the picture, a few developed, so were worth adding.

*Original Painting which was abandoned*

*Original Pencil sketch which was re-traced for second, completed picture*

Artist Code: 1404. Kingcup. Completed April 2014, Unframed Size: 12" x 16", Medium: Water colour. Used on poster design for Iceni Botanical Artists Annual Exhibition 2019.

# Song Thrushes in Ivy

Green, green the ivy clings, and climbs and bounds all over things
She sits amongst the leaves of green He sits above in spotted sheen
They flitter in and out of shade A bonded pair so cutely made.
The handsome Song Thrush looks so sweet, Yet thrashes with his weapon beak,
An unsuspecting snail in shell, Against a stone, and, you can tell,
He loves and gulps his juicy sprat, A garden pest gone just like that!
Although the air is cold and clear, and blue skies sometimes do appear
The thrush will seek a comfort nook, Amongst the ivy leaves, but look,
Some blackened berries still hang there, they'll pluck and eat till all is bare

After seeing two song thrushes confront one another and a blackbird lingering in the background, this little nonsense poem came to mind.

AND…A TALE OF THREE 'DICKIES'

Two little dickie-birds sitting on a stump,
On the edge of their patch they met with a bump
'What brings you here?' the first one said
'This is my patch you know, so leave or your
    dead!'
The other one said, 'You have so many snails,
There's plenty for both, so no need for flails'
The first one said, 'I'm in no mood to share
So buzz off you stranger, be off, so there'
The other one said, 'But please be so kind
For your well being, and my peace of mind
Let's pool our resources, we'll catch more food
If we both stick together and face the feud'
But first-hand dickie was not going to crack
For manners and intellect sadly lacked
So as he argued with the intruder
Another dickie—who appeared to be ruder—
Was keenly eyeing the tasty meal
And down in a swoop the morsel did steal
So whilst the two dickies were squabbling away
Blackbird dickie made use of affray
Cackling his presence as he flew to his perch
Leaving two dickies quite left in the lurch!

Artist Code: 0703. Water colour (12" × 16", completed February 2007) Song Thrush, *Turdus philomelos*, Ivy, *Hedera helix*. Original sold at Holt Picturecraft Gallery, September 2009. My grateful thanks to Ian Dickerson whose perfectly cute photograph (lower Song Thrush) was the inspiration behind this compilation of thrushes in ivy in January.

# Brown Orchid: Zygopetalum

*Zygopetalum* a wonderful name
This lovely orchid's bridge to fame
A shimmering star of umber brown
And purple skirt gently billowing down
Swirling and curling, the textural bloom
To paint it complete—there was no room!

As mentioned previously, my neighbour, Alan, grows beautiful orchids and regularly hands them to me over the garden fence as they come into flower so that I can paint them in my studio. Because of a rush in other work matters, I had to paint this picture over two years; the flower heads in the first year, then the leaves and bulbs the second year. Fortunately, my initial and concise drawing meant that although the leaves had grown (a lot!), I was still able to depict the plant accurately.

The plant was quite large so, in order to fit the picture on to my normal 12" x 16" paper, I designed the layout in two halves, flowerheads on the left and the rest of the plant on the right, which makes a pleasing and balanced artwork.

Artist Code: 0801. Water colour (12" × 16", completed May 2008). This work was sold by the Darryl Nantais Gallery, Linton, Nr Cambridge, UK.

# Fritillaries and Dew Drops

The RHS so love this flora  
They really like its bell-shaped aura  
'Award of Garden Merit' gained  
This hardy native flower named  
With checkered pattern all bizarre  
From mauve to white this lovely flower  
Grows in grass or under shrubs  
Or proudly shows in giant tubs  
The purple bells 'sing' with the lark  
The white ones have a 'watermark'  
Extremely hardy, trouble-free  
In splendour grow for all to see (*except when the Lily beetle comes!*)

I offered an original 'painting of choice' as an auction prize for a ball held to raise money for the premature baby unit at the Rosie Maternity Hospital (Cambridge), which my youngest son and daughter-in-law were helping to organize. (I felt guilty for not also helping, as I was on holiday in Spain!) The ball raised over £6,000.

The winner of my donated prize decided that she would like a painting of the fritillaries growing in her garden (the original eight bulbs of which came from Scotland). When I visited her home, the feast of flowers dotted all over her large garden left me in awe. I was allowed to pick as many as I liked, and when I suggested that the tulip-like fritillaries also growing in her garden would make a nice back-drop against the snakeshead ones, I picked an armful of those also. It is one of the hardest paintings I have done—but it was one very happy and contented prize-winner.

The winner dug up a few bulbs and gave them to me which I planted in my little wild garden. They have been flowering regularly, but each year I am plagued by the non-native Red Lily beetle. So each year I go out hunting as the flower buds form to remove any beetles and larvae, because that is the time they seem to destroy the plant. This invasive species is now widespread in England and Wales, and was found in Scotland in 2002, and as recently as 2010 in the Republic of Ireland.

Artist Code: 1108. Water colour (12" × 16", completed April 2008). Snakeshead fritillaries—*Fritillaria meleagris*, Bell fritillaries—*Fritillaria michailovskyi*.

The alien Lily beetle (*Lilioceris lilii*) is a great pest to lilies, reducing a plant to nothing in only a few days.

# Bird of Paradise

Gorgeous tassels, blue and gold  
The 'birds of paradise' unfold  
With crimson sheath, unfurling fronds  
The blade of leaf together bonds  
This wondrous plant will stir the heart  
Like lovers who will never part

A few bits of flora and fauna painted whilst on holiday at Casa Olivia. And see 'Canoodling in the Loquats' next page.

I was on holiday in Spain in early July 2004, and these beautiful clumps of flowers were growing in the terraced garden. I had taken my painting equipment with me to finish off a couple of paintings, but every time I went outside the beauty of these orange and blue starlets haunted me. With permission of the owner of the property (my lovely sister) I cut them and placed them carefully in the middle of my clothes in the suitcase and hoped they would not be damaged in flight. Hardy things, they remained in perfect condition until I had finished my painting back home in England. This painting was featured in the local *Cambridge Evening News* described as an 'exquisite picture of an exotic plant'.

Here are some pictures of the lovely house where I had my wonderful Spanish holiday, a beautifully secluded old farmhouse in an old olive grove valley, situated within a golf course in Cortijo Grande, Nr Ture, Spain. A haven for botanical and natural history artists. The house is now called 'Cortijo del Guarda' (formerly Casa Olivia).

Artist Code: 0001. *Strelitzia*. Life-size oil painting on stretched canvas (22" × 18", completed September 2004). Original sold to private collector, September 2005.

# Canoodling in the Loquats

Sunny yellow, blackbird size  
The Oriole to England flies  
to Lakenheath, its favourite spot  
though doesn't pose for photo-shot  
But escapades in Spain are here  
Enjoyed, and bringing morning cheer  
Soon loquat fruits will ripe and fall  
And youngsters from the nest will call  

This was the second of my artworks to be featured as 'Picture of the Month' in the Portfolio section of the printed *Artists & Illustrators Magazine*, October 2011 issue. ('Passion Flower Bits' was featured in Portfolio in the March 2010 issue). Also selected for the National Exhibition of Wildlife Art (NEWA) 2012. Catalogue Number 49, with picture feature. From 2010 to 2014 this painting was available as a Wentworth Whimsy Jigsaw Puzzle from www.jigsaws.co.uk, Catalogue no. 592306. It was very nice to receive royalties on sales!

At Cortijo del Guarda (formerly Casa Olivia), Cortijo Grande, Spain, in late May 2011, every morning at dawn my family were awoken by the distinctive fluting whistle of Golden Orioles. As we stumbled inelegantly and speedily out of bed, we were lucky to see the birds feasting on the ripe Loquat fruits (*Eriobotrya japonica*). In between pecking at the fruit they were chasing each other about—obviously pre-nuptials. We were so lucky that a flock of Orioles stopped off in the valley. The first day of our holiday, we saw 8 birds. By the end of the week there was only a solitary male, so this was 'right place, right time'! The best place to see Orioles in the UK is Lakenheath Nature Reserve (East Anglia), which I visited once and heard one calling, but never caught a glimpse. Even though they are this beautiful rich yellow, they are extremely difficult to spot amongst the foliage. But what beautiful birds; and loquats make a fine jam!

In May 2013 my husband and I revisited the house and this time watched a pair of Golden Orioles building their nest in a Eucalyptus tree during the week we were there. I actually captured on film their mating ritual which was most exciting and very noisy (see nest photographs below—main part made from a polythene bag).

Artists Code 1107. Water colour painting (12" × 16", completed August 2011). Golden Orioles—*Oriolus oriolus*, Loquats—*Eriobotrya japonica*). The original was sold at the National Exhibition of Wildlife Art (NEWA) 2012.

# Roe Deer and Fawn at Fullers Mill

What a beautiful place, tucked away in the middle of a forest in the wilds of Suffolk, East Anglia, UK. I travelled to Fullers Mill on 16th May 2018 meeting up with the Iceni Botanical Artists (IBA) Group, of which I am a member, and we had a great day painting and drawing. Bernard Tickner, local hero for Lackford Lakes Nature Reserve, and one-time master brewer, owned and lived at Fullers Mill for many years and built up the garden in his own fashion, collecting plants from all over the world with his wife, Bess. Bernard outlived his wife to the age of 93, passing away in November 2017. The IBA decided to honour Bernard's life and contribution to the preservation of nature with a series of paintings of the Fullers Mill Garden and its plants. These paintings were shown, with other floral artworks, at the IBA exhibition, Apex, Bury St Edmunds 14th August to 9th September 2018.

This painting is the work of my day at Fullers Mill (16th May 2018) which included partaking of the delicious cake and coffee available from the little cafe, as well as purchasing Bernard's Book: A Scratch in the Soil relating his life and times. A fascinating and entertaining read, with all proceeds from the sale of the book going towards the upkeep of the gardens for the nation. I walked around the gardens several times with camera in hand, but mostly just to take in the varied vistas, from the River Lark which runs right through, to the almost dried (on the day) Mill Pond, the large lake at the back of the garden and all the different flowers and plants. It was an extremely cold day and most of the other artists went home before lunchtime. But I stuck it out till close at 5.00pm because I was playing in a tennis match at Newmarket on my way home, so no point leaving early. I did a few flower drawings using my Polychromos oil pencils, but mostly just enjoyed the atmosphere, the flowers and the wildlife.

In January 2022, the Iceni Botanical Artists decided that their next botanical project would be to paint a year of the flora and fauna in Fullers Mill Garden. After discussions with the Head Gardener, and permission from the Perennial Charity (who now look after the garden), it was decided that it should be a two-year project with completion of all artworks set for 1st January 2024. We will also be publishing a book of selected artworks from the project, hopefully to coincide with our Annual Art Exhibition.

The Head Gardener kindly supplied the IBA with a list of plants which grow in the garden and which she felt would be appropriate for our project; animals, birds, insects, and fish, which live in or visit the garden were also included. Iceni Artists have been free to choose which plants, vistas and fauna they would like to depict, so there are a few duplicates—but not many, and in very different styles.

**My main task for the project is to paint 12 snowdrops—some rare, some not so, and others which are different, for example, white and yellow flowers and parts, rather than white and green.**

**At the publishing date of this book (August 2023) I have painted seven of my 12 snowdrops (*Galanthus*), four of which are shown here over the next few pages, along with a Star Magnolia (*Magnolia stellata*). and a Harlequin Glory Bower (*Clerodendrum trichotomum*). Other paintings to be done include Garlic mustard with Orange tip butterfly and caterpillar, Silver Birch (*Betula* 'Silver Grace'), Otter, alien Signal Crayfish (with water plants), Grey wagtail, Water vole, rabbits and squirrels—though completion of these will totally depend upon other commitments.**

Artist Code: 1804. Completed 25th July 2018. Original water colour 16" x 12", Saunders Waterford Classic hot pressed cotton rag 140lbs.

# Fullers Mill, West Stow, Suffolk
# Iceni Botanical Artists Project
# to paint a year at Fullers Mill Garden

## Galanthus 'Queen Olga'

This painting is the first of the 12 snowdrops on my Fullers Mill list of works to be done, which is the earliest flowering of the year but is strange in that only the flowers and stems grow first, then the leaves grow once the seed heads have formed. You will notice on the right of this painting that the snowdrops and stems have no leaves, and on the left, amongst the leaves which grow November–December, the seed heads have developed — the flowers being long gone. It was nice to be able to depict the bulbs as well, but some of the plants amongst the 12 are quite rare so this will not be possible in those instances.

FLOWERS SEPTEMBER, OCTOBER

Other names: Queen Olga's snowdrop, Autumn snowdrop, *Galanthus nivalis* subsp. *reginae-olgae*, *Galanthus corcyrensis*

*Galanthus reginae-olgae* has revolute leaves that are dark green with a central silver line and when fully grown are 11–15 cm long by 3–8 mm wide. Its flowers have three larger outer tepals, pure white, and three smaller inner tepals, white with variable green markings near the tips. The outer tepals are about 15–35 mm long, the inner ones 9–12 mm in length.

Artist Code 2209. *Galanthus* Queen Olga (*Galanthus reginae-olgea*). Water colour on Aquarelle Arches 100% cotton paper 140lb. 10" x 14". Completed 12th December 2022.

# Galanthus 'Three Ships'

This painting is the second of the 12 snowdrops. Sadly, as this one is quite rare, I was unable to have sight of the bulbs. But I hope the character of this 'bulbous' snowdrop and its 'chunky' short leaves, growing amongst the withering oak leaves, shows well in the painting so that it can be identified. Magnified sections of the plant's particular flower patterns are shown—completely different from the Queen Olga, the first painting in the series.

FLOWERS AS EARLY AS DECEMBER AT CHRISTMAS

'Three Ships' is a clump-forming, bulbous perennial with broadly-strap-shaped, greyish-green leaves and flowers produced in early winter, this cultivar is often in flower by Christmas day. The rounded flowers have heavily-textured white outer segments and flared inner segments with broad green markings at the base and an inverted V-shaped marking at the apex *Galanthus plicatus* subsp. *byzantinus* 'Three Ships'.

Artist Code 2212. Water colour on Aquarelle Arches 100% cotton paper 140lb 10" x 14". Completed 4th January 2023.

# Galanthus 'Richard Ayres'

This is the third in a series of 12 paintings of snowdrops for the IBA Fullers Mill Project. This startling flower, when you lift the head and peep below the petticoat of petals is stunning. There are quite a few variations in the number of outer petals and inner rings as well as the patterns on the inner sepals. Most intriguing.

*Galanthus* 'Richard Ayres' is a distinctive snow drop! At a visit to Anglesey Abbey, Cambridge in 1987, Richard Nutt noticed a very beautiful and unusual large, double snowdrop. Apparently it had been dug out of the wood to where all the snowdrops of the estate had been moved many years ago. It was named by the National Trust (the present owners of Anglesey Abbey), after the Head Gardener, Richard Ayres.

Artist Code 2301. Water colour on Aquarelle Arches 100% cotton paper 140lb. 10" x 14". Completed 20th January 2023.

# Galanthus 'gracilis'

This is the fourth in a series of 12 paintings of snowdrops for the IBA Fullers Mill Project. This slender, delicate flower, with twisted pencil leaves was not on the original list of 12. But another which was to be painted (*Galanthus jacquenetta*) failed to grow properly so I was asked to include the *gracilis* instead.

Although I decided to check the *Galanthus jacquenetta* this year (2023) and it was showing quite nicely. So I did some preliminary drawings and took some photographs—it may be added as number 13, if I get time to complete everything before 1st January 2024 which is the completion date for all artworks for the project.

*Galanthus gracilis* is a distinctive garden plant with twisted, glaucous narrow leaves. Both the plant and its flowers are smaller than most snowdrop species.

FLOWERS LATE WINTER, EARLY SPRING.

Artist Code 2302. Water colour on Aquarelle Arches 100% cotton paper 140lb. 10" x 14". Completed 1st March 2023.

# Magnolia stellata 2

Another painting for the Fullers Mill project, started in January 2023, thinking I had enough time to complete it before my snowdrops emerged. However, I was wrong; so, having used sketches drawn on tracing paper from the first time I painted this lovely plant, and adding a couple more flowers and a spray of autumnal leaves, I had to put it on the back burner. It came out to be completed 10th March and I completed it 21st March 2023. I have called it 'Magnolia stellata 2' because my previous painting, done in 2010 was called 'Magnolia stellata', but was a special one with a silver ring included in the design to celebrate the 25th anniversary of the Society of Botanical Artists. It was one of a trio of magnolias painted on a dark blue wash, using the background to create the subtle greys and blues of the shady parts (see below). Sadly, they were not selected for the 2010 SBA exhibition, but nevertheless, I sold them at subsequent exhibitions elsewhere.

**All three of the paintings (left) have a silver ring which is metallic ink on a raised gesso base. The backgrounds are blue water colour washes; flowers and leaves are water colour. I did not mix enough blue background paint to cover all three 9" x 12" sheets, so just made three different shades of blue!**

*Magnolia grandiflora.* Artist Code: 1004. Completed January 2010. Watercolour on Aquarelle Arches 100% hot pressed cotton rag paper. Unframed size 9" x 12".

Framed Size 13" x 15". Sold to a private collector. I had put much white body paint over the blue background on this painting, which cracked a little, so I did not sell it originally, but offered it at a reduced price and the buyer was happy with the 'damaged' surface.

Splendid Magnolia (my name for it as the variety was unknown). Artist Code: 1005. Completed January 2010. Water colour on Aquarelle Arches 100% hot pressed cotton rag paper. Unframed size 9" x 12".

Sold at Monday Art Group Exhibition, Comberton Village Hall, July 2010.

Many thanks to my lovely neighbour, Alan, who allowed me to pluck the live specimens from the tree in his front lawn.

*Magnolia stellata.* Artist Code: 1006. Completed February 2010. Watercolour on Aquarelle Arches 100% hot pressed cotton rag paper. Unframed size 9" x 12".

Sold at Monday Art Group Exhibition, Comberton Village Hall, July 2010.

A ring of silver round the branch,
For botanic anniversary launch,
The SBA* has over time,
Provided floral art so fine,
Selected pictures hold the grades,
Their painted beauty never fades

*Society of Botanical Artists*

Artist Code 2304. Star Magnolia. Water colour on Aquarelle Arches 100% cotton paper 140lb. 12" x 16". Completed 21st March 2023.

# Clerodendrum trichotomum 'Purple Blaze'

Whilst I was sketching and collecting data for my first snowdrop painting under the Fullers Mill Project mentioned previously, the Head Gardener approached me to ask if I would consider doing an extra plant which she thought should be added to the plant list already supplied.

I was asked me to paint this Harlequin Glory Bower, so I said I would do it. A small sprig was plucked from the large bushy shrub which was an invaluable resource during the picture painting. I did not have access to the live flowers so had to rely on photographs. The beautiful star-shaped seed heads are painted at three times magnification but the lower part of the painting is life-size.

The plant originates from western China and puts on a good show all year round. In spring, it has fresh green foliage with purple tips and during summer it bears clusters of pinky buds which turn into creamy-white scented flowers.

The plant here shows the steel-blue fruits surrounded by a dusky pink–maroon calyx which form after the summer flowering. In late autumn the leaves turn butter yellow and drop, but the 'stars' remain on the bare branches far into winter.

Artist Code 2208. Harlequin Glory Bower. Water colour on Aquarelle Arches 100% cotton rag paper 140lb. 10" x 14". Completed 4th November 2022

# Little Explorers at the Mini Mart

With petals five in roundel form,
The brightest green on any dawn
Beware its hidden dangers for,
'Tis poisonous Stinking Hellebore
But revel in the bell-like beauty,
Tamed in medicine in its duty.
Little explorers on the mini trolley
Have no need for commercial 'lolly'
the mini basket makes a perch
While all the time they are on a search
To pick up insects to feed their brood
A family bird which shares its food

The backdrop to this painting was a scene from the bottom of my little wild garden. The mini shopping trolley was used as the base to a flower wreath at my dear mother's funeral in 2007 because she just loved supermarket shopping.

There was a wild honeysuckle growing through it, as well as privet. The stinking hellebore was in a pot ready to be planted in the little wild garden. Unfortunately, it died before it could be planted out. I purchased it to replace one which had grown up naturally—which had disappeared. Apparently these plants are fertilized by snails (of which there are still plenty in my little garden), but obviously the blackbirds, thrushes and hedgehog (in 2020 extinct in my garden) must have eaten all the snails so that the hellebore lost its source for procreation.

We usually feed the birds, and the long-tailed tits which visit are only interested in the peanuts, but also flit about amongst the myriad young trees I have planted, including exploring all the pieces of old wood scattered about, as well as the shopping trolley, searching for insects which they love. They sometimes like to eat seeds late in the year. This lovely little bird is very sociable and you cannot fail to distinguish their little busy, twittering calls as they fly in familial flocks from one garden to another. The young of a first litter even help the parents feed and bring up a later brood, so a gorgeous little bird all round.

I had taken this freshly painted picture (completed the day before) to a 'Meet the Artist' day at Hinchingbrooke Country Park where I was exhibiting. I placed it unframed, unmounted on my table, along with another newly completed work, for people to look at. Two wonderful individuals came along and purchased the paintings—these were my quickest sales at the time!

Artist Code 1506. Long tailed tits, *Aegithalos caudatus*, Stinking hellebore *Helleborus foetidus*. Original Water colour on Aquarelle Arches 100% cotton rag. Completed 13 August 2015. Unframed size 9" x 12".

# A House in Provençe

A commission to show sweet lavender blue
Which complements the bright sky hue
Showing sunshine, at noon-day clock
And shimmering, varied hollyhock
The shutters then provide cool shade
Hark, distant whisper of turbine blade

This painting was completed using various photographs supplied by the commissioners. I was asked to portray this picture in a particular style, i.e. typical soft watercolour and pen and ink outlining. But once I had applied the 'soft' water colour, with the colours being so vibrant, I felt that the painting did not need an ink outline, and the commissioners agreed. A typical house in Provençe, with lavender field. A beautiful landscape.

Commission. Artist Code: 1002. Completed December 2009. Water colour on Aquarelle Arches 100% hot pressed cotton rag paper. Unframed size 12" x 16".

# Three New Blades

We love to have the visitors here  
Who share the spoils with mice and deer  
In brilliant flocks they scan each hedge  
Pluck and plunder—life on the edge  
Then hedgerows stripped but none bemoan  
The little beggars just go back home!

This little painting was 'Highly Commended' in The Artist and Leisure Painter TALP Open 2020 gallery exhibition:

'17th June 2020: Congratulations! One or more of your entries has been highly commended! The highly-commended works, along with the full exhibition will be shown online at www.painters-online.co.uk from 10am on 9 July 2020, when the prize winners will also be announced. Due to the Coronavirus unprecedented global crisis, the galleries at Patchings Art Centre are temporarily closed, which is why we are unable to stage The Artist and Leisure Painter TALP Open 2020 gallery exhibitions. We look forward to returning to our normal competition, gallery exhibitions and festival format in 2021. Thank you for your participation in our competition, and many congratulations on your success.'

I started this little painting way back in 2016 after receiving permission to use some lovely resource photographs of Fieldfare and Redwing from Paul Mason and Simon Stirrup. The backdrop resource was my own photograph taken at Christmas in Lincolnshire when I was staying with my eldest son. His garden was full of fallen apples and twigs and the frost was just beginning to melt on the debris around. I felt the two things would go together nicely. On this frosty Lincolnshire morning there were a few little blades of bright green grass poking through amongst the winter debris which inspired the title of the work.

However, after I had just completed the drawing, which incidentally I rather bravely drew from scratch with a paintbrush and paint instead of a pencil, several commissions came in and other publishing work so I had to put this particular painting on hold. I forgot all about it until January 2020—it took just over four years to complete!

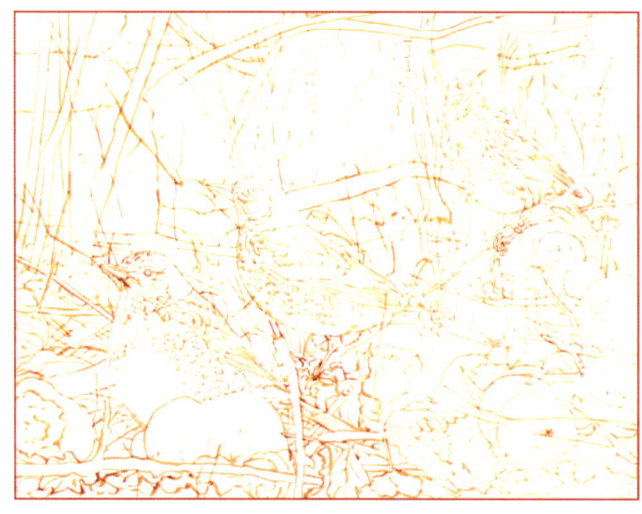

*Original painted sketch from 2016*

I uploaded the finished painting to my website shop and it sold overnight! The buyers visited the studio and we had tea and cakes on the patio (all distanced though because of the COVID rules) and off it went to its new home in Suffolk, UK.

Artist Code: 1604. Completed 9th March 2020. Fieldfares and Redwing. Sold April 2020 to private buyer. Water colour on Aquarelle Arches 100% hot pressed cotton rag. Unframed size 12" x 9".

# Dahlia: Bishop of Llandaff

Of bishop red this dahlia fine,
expressive curves with so straight line
A bulging bud, a flower peak,
voluptuous red knows how to 'speak'

I am a firm believer in Continued Professional Development (CPD) and regularly attend botanical art refresher courses at Cambridge University Botanic Gardens with different tutors. In September 2021, I enrolled in a class to paint Autumn flowers. There were so many plants to choose from that I was quite in a quandary.

However, I kept harking back to the beautiful shape and colour of this Dahlia and, when I learned its name 'Bishop of Llandaff', it became even more intriguing—so my choice was made.

Trying to complete a botanical artwork in three days never works for me, so I had to do as much as time would allow and hope that I had enough colour drafts of each piece of the plant and a good memory to enable me to complete the work in due course.

Upon its reappearance on my itinerary of artworks in March 2022, I became aware that the original drawing, which was traced and put onto my lovely water colour paper during the course seemed slightly unbalanced. So I added an extra stem and flower (the central stalk and top left flower and buds) which rendered the composition more likeable!

So it all came to fruition nicely in March 2022, after its inception and brief workings started in September 2021!

Artist Code 2204. Started 7 September 2021, completed 3rd March 2022. ORIGINAL Water colour on Aquarelle Arches 100% Cotton Rag, 140lbs 12" x 16".

This was one of the live flowers which I used to design my painting. I had to rely on photographs to complete it.

# *Golden Pheasants and Bluebells*

Golden Pheasants, plumage so fine  
On nuts and berries and insects dine  
Little hen in shadows waits  
Till intruder leaves—so long it takes  
But partner cock is ready and brave  
Be off with you, you insolent knave!

The inspiration for the background in this painting popped into my head whilst I was walking in May 2015 with a group of caravanning friends in the beautiful British countryside (Cotswolds I think) and we came across a small wooded glade with bluebells and young green, spring plants growing with the morning sun glinting through the gaps in the trees and hedgerows. There was an old wooden stump covered with moss and tree seedlings dotted about. It really was a beautiful scene. I had not taken my camera so am indebted to my friend, Martin, who allowed me to use his and I took some lovely photographs of the scene and surrounds.

The very next week I went to Kew Gardens for the first time in my life (with my camera this time), and there I met up with some gorgeous Golden Pheasants. I snapped to my hearts content, thinking all the time that they would go beautifully with the bluebell background.

It has taken me from 2015 to 24th June 2020 to complete this work, which took 82 hours to paint (not counting the preliminary thinking and drawing rounds).

Golden Pheasants, much slighter than 'normal' ones, are around in the wild in the UK, but rare as their bright plumage makes them susceptible to death by wily fox! They can be seen all year round in small areas of England, Scotland and Wales, in forests and dense woodlands.

Artist Code: 1515. Picture inception 2015. Drawing done 20th June 2018. Painting started 10th May 2020, completed 24th June 2020. Original Water colour. Aquarelle Arches 140lb 100% cotton rag paper, 12" x 16". Sold to private collector July 2020.

This is the original background photograph taken in 2015 whilst out walking.

# Iris bucharica (Corn Leaf Iris)

As happens with quite a few of my paintings, this artwork began its life at a CPD refresher course at Cambridge University Botanic Gardens in April 2013. As mentioned earlier, I never manage to complete a piece during the actual course, so this one was put on the back burner for later production.

Whilst checking through all my drafts of botanical work (all waiting to be completed) I came across this draft again in March 2022. Most times I make enough thorough and precise notes in pencil, colour, and writing, to be able to accurately complete a work at a later date. However, when I started working on this one, I realised that there was not enough precise information in my notes and sketches to work out some of the detail.

I had written down that this plant grows in Afghanistan and that its name was *Iris bucharica* (or Corn Leaf Iris), but my failure to attend to the important points of the leaf axil joints and writing down how many petals in the flowers and how they sit together was a really large omission.

So the finished article has involved some artistic license (or guesswork), for which I apologise. So I would not deem this to be an accurate 'Botanical Illustration'—more a 'Flower Painting'. But it is a really beautiful, if slightly different, Iris, and quite small due to its harsh growing environment in Afghanistan. The leaves in particular differ from your normal Iris leaves and I love their 'curly-whirlies'.

Artist Code 2205. Started April 2013, completed 9th March 2022. ORIGINAL Water colour on Aquarelle Arches 100% Cotton Rag, 140lbs 10" x 14".

# Love at First Sight

Love at first sight, fluorescent blue
Red underbill is the female clue
The male has an all black bill to see
And you won't find him sitting in a tree
Rivers and wetlands are this bird's home
Amongst the reeds they like to roam

Brief was to use photograph supplied by commissioner and add kingfishers and daisies. The photograph had been taken on a very dull day and the background water was a really dark grey. I added kingfishers—nice bright birds and likely to be by the water, and the daisies added a nice white contrast to the work. I also lightened the dark background (artistic licence). When the commissioner saw it she acknowledged that I had done exactly what was asked of me. But she had changed her mind about adding kingfishers and daisies to the original photograph and asked if I would mind doing it again—just copying the supplied photograph exactly.

The resource photograph had been taken by the commissioner's grandson which had won a prize at school. So I did another painting in just water colour (Artist Code 2002, below and titled it 'Regeneration—The Mighty Reed', completed 30 January 2020), and she was delighted with the result. The painting was a gift for her daughter's 50th birthday.

I was very fortunate, and grateful, that the commissioner liked the kingfisher picture too and purchased that one for herself.

Below is the resource photograph taken by the grandson (left) and the completed second artwork (right)

Commission. Artist Code 2001. Kingfishers, Reeds and Daisies. Completed 2nd January 2020. Original water colour, oil pencil and Acrylic. Aquarelle Arches 100% cotton rag 140lb paper 16" x 12".

# Prunus 'Mirabelle'

This little painting was a successful submission to the Association of Botanical Artist's (ABA) December 2022 Online Exhibition 'Beauty in the Detail' (December 2022 to May 2023). A pre-requisite for the exhibition was to draw a large version of a particular plant or part of it with scale bars (see below), which had to fit on a 25cm x 25cm sheet.

The story behind the painting is that I played in a golf match at Haverhill golf club in June 2022 and dropped my distance glasses somewhere on the course. I left my details with the pro shop and it was remarkable that someone found them a few days later and the professional in the shop posted them to me.

The found glasses at Haverhill had unfortunately been run over by a trolley! However, the lenses were still intact so I took the broken frame and good lenses to a mender of such things at Over (Cambs). I had found an old pair of specs and asked if my lenses could be fitted to the old frame. The answer was 'Yes' but that it would take about 20 minutes. So to kill time I went for a little walk towards the centre of Over village. As I walked towards the village pond, these plums shone out of the thick hedgerow and I thought how beautiful they were. I took some photographs of the pond and on my way back decided to pluck a few small branches of plums from the hedgerow and used them to design and paint the artwork.

(Ironically, in May 2022, I again lost my glasses on the golf course, not noticing that they had fallen from my trolley after removing them to take off my jumper, at my new home golf Club (Girton, previously Bourn), and was lucky again that someone found them a few days later—this time still all intact with just a tiny scratch near the top rim of the left lens. So I have vowed now never to wear glasses whilst playing golf!)

*Prunus* 'Mirabelle' painting showing the pencilled in scale bars. Designing this painting onto a 25cm x 25cm sheet was quite difficult as square artwork does not fit nicely in my mind's eye, and I found it to be more of a challenge than expected.

Artist Code 2206. Yellow plum. Water colour on Aquarelle Arches 100% cotton rag paper 140lb. 25cm x 25cm. Completed 27th July 2022.

# I Bow to my Queen

I bow to my Queen; I'm all on the lean
Will she be proud; her head in the cloud
Can love be rejected; please hear me my love
I'm down here dejected, whilst you're up above (SWLK)

In October 2020 I was asked to produce an artwork of turtle doves for someone's 80th birthday. As there was only a week between commissioning and the birthday, all I could manage was a pencil sketch, although the recipient was very pleased with the result (see Artist Code 2016 below*).

I was so taken with the commissioned pencil sketch that I felt impelled to make a colour version, albeit executed on a more leisurely timetable. So it took 4 months to complete! But when it was complete, I was not happy with it. I laid it aside for a time then looked at it again—the birds were not colourful enough so I reworked the painting in August 2021 and felt much happier about it all.

Turtle doves have so many colours, many of which are indistinct nuances rather than distinguishable colours. I have exercised my artistic license in portraying these beautiful birds in early, bright morning sunlight so the colours are arbitrary. Resources for this work are my own photographs taken at Pensthorpe Nature Reserve in Norfolk a few years ago. The doves and other wild fowl, including Bearded tits/reedlings (subject of another artwork: Artist Code 2012), were in a very large aviary, and the birds were acting as near-normal as can be in such circumstances. Ruffs were cavorting, and the male turtle doves were parading—hence the title. The background is a sawn tree-stump surrounded by wood anemones taken in Switzerland around 2010, but which could easily be in Britain, so I decided to use it!

Formerly this bird was often heard 'brrring' away in our English countryside. Now the sound is very rare. Turtle doves are on the UK Red List of species. The good news is that 'Operation Turtle Dove' is working closely with farmers by encouraging them to provide good habitat which suits the birds' needs, and there are other global organised conservation efforts which may help to stem their decline: 30 per cent loss in the 16 years up to October 2015 (so sad).

*Artist Code 2016. Commissioned 80th Birthday sketch which inspired the colour version.

Artist Code 2017. Original coloured version with paler birds.

Artist Code 2017. Turtle Doves. Started 29 November 2020 completed 23 April 2021). THEN REWORKED AUGUST 2021 (see right). Original water colour 12" x 16", Aquarelle Arches 140lb cotton rag paper.

# The Victorian Aviary Garden

ORIGINAL WATER COLOUR. Completed February 2010. Unframed size 16" x 12". Artist Code: 1007. COPYRIGHT © re-assigned to commissioner in writing (except for greetings cards). Brief: ARTISTS IMPRESSION for a 2010 Chelsea Flower Show Garden.

This angled, scaled painting was commissioned by PHILIPPA PEARSON, Garden and Landscape Designer, and her associate, JONATHAN DENBY. Philippa and Jonathan were selected for the first time to show a garden at the Chelsea Flower Show (2010), entitled, 'The Victorian Aviary Garden', which received a silver medal. This commission was painted using water colour. The brief was to design a scaled artist's impression of the garden, I spent much time on the internet getting to know the beautiful flowers that were planted in the garden, and produced my own little booklet containing guide sketches of the plants, with sizes and colours, which enabled me to make a reasonably accurate portrayal of the finished garden.

*The Victorian Aviary Garden Illumination*
ORIGINAL WATER COLOUR. Completed February 2010. Unframed size 16" x 12". Artist Code: 1008. Commissioned Illumination for publicity to complement the Artist's Impression of the 2010 Chelsea Flower Show Garden painting. This work was painted with water colour, gum arabic, and gold metallic powder. The brief was to design the illumination around the Victorian Aviary Garden design (Artist Code 1007, right), so that it would complement the garden illustration. The illumination was used to produce handouts at Chelsea, and the garden picture for publicity purposes, including being published in the 2010 RHS Flower Show catalogue. Invitation Cards were also printed for the event, using the artwork supplied.

2010 Chelsea Flower Show Garden
Artist Impression
by Tina Bone (Water colour)

The Victorian Aviary Garden
Designed by Phillipa Pearson
and Jonathan Denby

# Flame Lily
## (Gloriosa superba Rothschildiana)

A lantern shape when first it swells
From green to scarlet now unveils
Then rustic pink with pointed ends
The petals dance as flames that bend
Revealing hidden parts within
As blood-red petals with yellow curl
A shimmering corolla in a twirl
Too soon the flaming flowers fade
Their duty done once seeds are made

My neighbour grew this plant especially for me in 2008 because someone had asked me to paint one—although in the end they only wanted to purchase one greetings card—so I was left with a painting that I would not have painted in the normal run of works!

This scrambling plant can grow 5 cm a day. It is the national flower of Zimbabwe (where it is a protected species). The red flame-like petals flicker in even the slightest breeze, and the bright green, translucent, twirling leaves glisten in the sunlight. The flowers start as tight green buds, then open slightly like stripy lanterns. The leaves take a stranglehold on anything that touches their curly tips. The petals surge outwards like a star, then sweep upwards like a fire, and as they fade the petals flatten and bend and fold inwards. What a beautiful plant.

After my plant had finished flowering and the leaves died I thought it had completed its life-cycle. However, although I had planted another plant in the original compost in the pot it kept springing up in the pot for a few years, lacing itself all over the Stephanotis which I had purchased and re-potted for my mum as a Mother's Day present in 2007! The reason my mum did not receive it was because she sadly passed away a week before. It is still (August 2023) sitting on my stair window sill and flowers every year. As I walk upstairs the heady scent and glossy leaved plant reminds me of my lovely mum. The Flame lily has gone.

Botanical Illustration. Artist Code: 0808. Completed May 2008. Water colour on Aquarelle Arches 100% hot pressed cotton rag paper. Unframed size 12" x 16". SOLD—Cambridge Open Studios Exhibition in July 2015.

# The Frank Taylor Memorial Peace Garden Gardening World Cup 2010

ORIGINAL WATER COLOUR Completed September 2010. Unframed size 12" x 16". Artist Code: 1021. Nagasaki, Japan (Gardening for Peace) Saturday, 9th October to Sunday, 17th October 2010.

Brief was to produce an Artist's impression of a garden from a written statement, plant list, and commissioner's sketch. Photographs were provided of urns, ferns, stained glass windows as resource (rescued from a church and installed in the commissioner's allotment hut!) from which the alabaster angel figurine would be sculpted by another artist. All the flowers are white, with a few blood-red blooms. The white for peace and the red for the blood spilled in the Great War. Urgent requirement; completed in good time

## SLOW LIFE

ABOUT JONATHAN DENBY, GARDEN DESIGNER (Commissioner)

The idea of Slow Life is to take the principles of Slow Food, which are 'good, clean and fair', and extend them to life in general.
In the Lake District, the air is clean, the pace is slow and the atmosphere is calm. If we don't grow food ourselves, we can buy it in friendly small shops, where you know the quality is going to be the best.

# 'The Jay's Feather'

A tiny Jay's feather resting there  
Midst snail shells next to petals pair  
And in the glass receptacles shine  
Rhododendron and Anemones fine  
This feather was found upon the ground  
Near a Jay's most favourite mound  
An unexpected gift for me  
To use right here as filigree  


This is the second painting done on Royal Talens black paper. As I liked the Anemones in Artist Code 2013 (pink ones (see below), I decided to re-use my traced pencil sketch and do them in white, but also added a sprig of *Rhododendron* and some garden snail shells and, of course, the Jay's feather. I have lots of little specimen jars full of nature's critters and their remnants (all deceased in natural circumstances, I might add), including the hide of a hedgehog, a badger skull, and blue tit's nest which was ravaged by a cat's paw (very sad as all the babies were killed and one of the parents. All our nest boxes in the garden now have protective wire to stop that ever happening again. Ironically the other parent bird we believe was also killed, but this time by a Sparrowhawk. I also have another nest with baby blue tit skeletons after a colony of tree bees invaded the blue tits box and frightened off the parents. The bees then proceeded to make a nest for a little while, then left in free abandonment.

Artist Code 2104. *Rhododendron ponticum*, white Japanese Anemones, a Jay's feather, and garden snail shells. Completed 26 May 2021.ORIGINAL—Gouache on A3 Royal Talens van Gogh black water colour 100% cellulose paper 140lbs. SOLD 29 October 2022, private sale. This painting has gone off to join its 'sister' painting (Artist Code 2013). Lovely.

# Puffins and Thrift

*Fratercula arctica* such special little birds
Roam the seas with increasing girds
As fishy-food grounds are scarcer and poor
They fly ever onwards trying to find more
And then each year the call of fate
Draws them to land to find their mate
A lifelong friend who is met with a kiss
Apart for too long, but now in new bliss

The idea for this painting came about when I received an email from JHG Jigsaw Puzzle company (who make jigsaw puzzles of my work on my behalf) asking if I had any puffin paintings because the National Trust had enquired about a puffin jigsaw at a trade fair.

Unfortunately, the answer was 'No', as I had never seen a puffin in the flesh. But I then remembered that lots of kind people who *had* been lucky enough to have seen these beautiful little birds for real had given me permission to use their fabulous photographs as resources, so I thought about doing something – although of course it was too late for the National Trust enquiry.

This was in early February 2022, and on 31st July I managed to complete my 'puffin vision'! After watching television programmes and some videos, I was able to see how puffins react with one another and as a group— and this is what I hope is conveyed in the finished painting.

The name '*Fratercula*' is Latin for 'little brother', a reference to the black and white plumage of puffins, which resembles monastic robes.

I acknowledge with enormous thanks the resources and inspiration provided by the following people: Simon Stirrup, Jan and Andy Smith, Paul Mason, Colin Mayes, David Oates, and Lizzie Harper (whose extremely accurate botanical works gave me inspiration for the flora in the composition when no live material was available).

Artist Code 2207. Puffins and Thrift ('*Fratercula arctica* Antics'). Started 14th February and completed 31st July 2022. Aquarelle Arches 140lbs water colour 100% cotton rag paper 14" x 20"—quite large for a water colour artwork!

# The Mighty Reed with Fragility

A 'Whim in the Willows' extends to the Fens
Where Reedlings build nests, the mighty reed bends
On edges and out in still waters they grow
Shelter for bird life as new life they sow.
August mists roll over bog. A man is walking with his dog.
The reeds in gentle breezes sway. The safest place by night and day,
for migrants who may soon be gone, to distant lands for winter sun.

This painting was achieved with help from a book I purchased from a secondhand bookshop whilst on holiday in Cornwall in the 1980s: *A Field Guide to the Nests, Eggs and Nestlings of British and European Birds* by Colin Harrison. It was an invaluable resource for finding out about Bearded Reedlings and helped me construct a viable composition. Bearded Tits (*Panurus biarmicus*) are beautiful little birds but their lovely colours make them disappear amongst the reedbeds where they live and breed. Their unmistakable 'ping-chew' song can be clearly heard.

I painted this picture specially for Book 5 'REED: ON THE EDGE' in the River Friend Series of which I am co-author (with Sylvia M Haslam), editor, illustrator and publisher. It is Figure 1. The Reedlings nest low down in old reed and the nest is made by twisting old reeds and grasses round sturdy reed stems and lined with old reed flower heads which are downy and soft. The birds usually lay between 5 and 7 eggs in a clutch and can breed from May to early September.

My resources for the birds themselves were taken on a very cold day in April 2017 when I visited Pensthorpe Nature Reserve in Norfolk. I had a lovely walk around the reserve, and particularly liked the marsh boardwalk where golden marsh marigolds abounded. But the best and cosiest bit was inside the walk-in aviary where the Reedlings were flitting about. I got some really good snapshots.

I plucked the dried reeds from a small stand at road edge near Toft, Cambs where the Bourn Brook waters flood onto the road occasionally with storm spate; and the green (live) reeds from those growing on the golf course through which the Bourn Brook meanders, because the water level was negligible (and dry in some places) and I was able to scramble down and pick a few fresh reeds without getting my feet wet during my golfing round—what a root system; but that is another story!

There are many uses for reed, some of which go back thousands of years and in the early twenty-first century there seems to be a revival in the crafts associated with it. Britain's largest reed beds are in the Broads in Norfolk and the Somerset Levels, but these pale to insignificance when compared with the enormous reed beds in Europe and elsewhere where they cover many hectares. Mystical myths and legends abound in stories of old about reedbeds and marshlands—a really fascinating history for one aquatic plant.

Artist Code 2012. Bearded Reedlings with nest and eggs. Completed 7th August 2020. Original water colour on Aquarelle Arches 140lb 100% cotton rag, 14" x 10".

# Three Plucked Petals

Three plucked petals fading below, The rest of the posy is still a good show
Leaves start to yellow and stalks turn to red, Outside the others still grow in their bed
But inside and standing tall in the glass, Their beauty and colour will now start to pass
But whilst standing tall, pink, and petite, This flower does well amongst the elite

I began working on this painting in September 2020 and it nearly went into the bin then! I had purchased some black water colour paper to try (A3 Royal Talens van Gogh black water colour 100% cellulose paper). It was on offer and once I started working on it I realised why it was less than half price!

For someone like myself, who paints very nitty-gritty, 100 per cent cellulose paper is like painting on rough bricks. Not good at all for botanical work for which I usually use hot pressed 100 per cent cotton rag (although I thought flowers on a black background would be lovely to do, ever since I saw a painting at Kew Gardens in Dr Shirley Sherwood's Gallery of a pink rhododendron on a black background, but painted on calf-skin vellum. It was so vibrant I determined that day that I would do a similar painting sometime). The rest of this black paper has been relegated to the bottom of the pile, way below my lovely Aquarelle Arches.

In summer 2020 I played tennis at Cambridge Lawn Tennis club where I am a member and there were a few pink Japanese anemones still flowering in the border around courts 1 and 2, so I asked permission to pick a few. I came home all excited with my prize and could not wait to get started. However, after sketching out my drawing on white paper to transfer onto the black stuff I realised that I did not know how to transfer a drawing onto black paper! In the end I managed to scan the sketch and print it on to the paper with a very feint green line. When I started painting with water colour, I was devastated that the paint just seemed to 'roll about' and disappear! I tried with oil pencils, but that did not look good, and then with acrylic: better, but still not the effect I was seeking. Very disillusioned, I cleaned my palette and put the painting away.

I turned again to the 'black paper' at the start of the January 2021 COVID lockdown, and re-drew the picture with white gouache and paintbrush. This worked very well, so I purchased a few gouache colours and set to work. This painting is the result.

*The purchaser of this original painting sent this beautiful photograph on 19 August 2021 mentioning that the flowers in his garden looked 'nearly as good as the painting' — lovely!*

Artist Code 2013. Japanese Anemones, *Anemone hupehensis*. Started September 2020 on black paper completed 12 January 2021. ORIGINAL — Gouache A3 Royal Talens van Gogh black water colour 100% cellulose paper 140lbs. SOLD 13 January 2021 Private Sale.

# Horrid Or Torrential

## A brook in transit the meandering Bourn

I trickled up from down below, where pure and pristine waters flow,
And bubbling in to light and sun, my source from Eltisley does run.
From ten miles west of Cambridge Town, where scholars toil in flowing gown,
Two hundred feet above the sea, with four in number tribut'ry,
Called Eastern Brook and Gascote Dean and Crow and Hay Deans too are seen.
Near Caxton village ancient 'lode', pointing north the Roman Road.
Called Ermine Street its way now crossed, the spoils of empire's myst'ries lost.
Then footpath hugs my pleasing banks, through village Bourn my entrance flanks.
And fording over Caxton End, I speed on with meandering bend.
For 'Bourn' means 'brook' it takes the name, to you or me it means the same!
And on and on passed football ground, and Doctors' surgery can be found.
I slip right through the village folds, as tees and greens my route beholds.
Where stood before great fields of corn, now shouts of 'Fore' are loudly borne.
Caldecote now comes to sight, and there I see a shimmering light,
As Dean Brook's waters swish and sway, and slink inside me on my way.
Next Toft with grazing fields of green, I mark its bound'ry, though I'm keen,
To tell you that with time these change, as my meanders morph in range.
More shouts of 'Fore' as on I chase, Meridian line does cross my face,
And probing distant stars and moons, the Mullard Dishes sing their tunes.
I form the watery binding space of Comberton/Barton's southern face.
And just beyond old Foxes Bridge, from furrowed field and stony ridge,
Sweet Tit Brook chuckles into view and brings sweet waters all anew,
But scampers right across my girth to join with Long Brook in its mirth
Then on and on, I am northern rim to Eversdens'/Haslingfield's country inns.
And on to Grantchester, meadows sweet, passed M11's noisy street.
I swoon 'neath widened bridge of road, no room here for Green Cross Code!
As traffic thunders all time long, you cannot hear my rippling song.
My deepest waters, bank so wide, where all the water creatures hide.
From run-off pipes now mainly fed, with hope that 'harmfuls' are all dead.
In Grantchester's historic place, near Byron's Pool, my 'Sense of Place'.
Is it 'Rhee' or 'Granta' where I am, or is it the gentle, flowing, 'Cam'?
As seawards rills envelope me, my Water's Spirit now runs free.

www.ingramcontent.com/pod-product-compliance
Lightning Source LLC
Chambersburg PA
CBRC100222100526
44590CB00008B/143